Apocalypse Later

A guide to the end of the world

by

Nice Mr Death

Edited by Mark Speed

TO ALEX AND VICKI,

BEST WISHES!

Nice Mr Death

Published by Terra Supra Limited
Registered in England and Wales no. 8109753

www.terrasupra.co.uk
Nothing is black and white

Printed and bound by CPI Group (UK) Ltd,
Croydon, CR0 4YY

For the avoidance of doubt, this is a satirical work.
www.endshow.com

To the boss

GOD

The free will thing was a nice idea.

Sorry it didn't pan out...[1]

[1] Of course you knew it wouldn't.. All these years of working for you and I still don't understand your ways.

Contents

Apocalypse Later[1]

If the world comes to an end, I want to be in Cincinnati. Everything comes there ten years later.

Mark Twain (1835 – 1910)

writer

S ome of the stunts described herein are dangerous and should not be tried at home. Or even in a place that is not your home or anyone else's home.

These stunts will be possible, just once, at the end of the world. Bathing in white-hot liquid metal prior to the End Time would be fatal, for example. It will, of course, be fatal at the end of the world too – but in a very different way. The kind of way where it doesn't matter.

[1]Apocalypse means 'revelation'. You've learnt something new already.

Introduction

I'm not afraid of death. I just don't want to be there when it happens.

Woody Allen (1935 –)
writer and director

This book was not written to offend. It was written to educate, entertain and to provoke thought and debate.

Let me introduce myself. My name is Nice Mr Death. I'm the guy who takes you from where you are when you die, to where you're going in the afterlife. I'm not a trickster, and I can't kill people – you're either dead or you're not. Where you're going after you die is entirely up to you and your beliefs.

I'm on a mission from God

God created Heaven and the Earth. He then had an enormous Sunday lunch and fell asleep for a very long time indeed. He woke up at the start of 2011 and wasn't best-pleased. The problem was this: you humans had gone off and created all these different religions – thousands of them. He doesn't mind that much, because they all lead back to Him. What does concern Him is that – with the end of the world approaching – you all have these different End Times. Heaven, Hell and Purgatory are, quite honestly, in desperate need of refurbishment. With over seven billion people we need to know how big to build each one. Furthermore, we can't have you all demanding different endings when it comes

9

to the crunch[1]. From my point of view this is also the last big job I do before I retire, so I want to get it right.

We did have some management consultants up from Hell for the day to give us advice[2]. They talked all this rubbish about streamlining, rebranding, business process re-engineering. Back to Hell they went...

But we did learn about *focus groups*. So God asked me to use the Edinburgh Fringe to run a series of focus groups[3]. I presented several different religions and got the audience to choose one. He asked me to do it again in 2012, and follow it up with this book to educate a wider public. By the way – I don't get commission from any of these religions. The choice is entirely yours – I just want you to be happy when you die.

This is my own personal guide to the End of the World. Remember to read the small print carefully – forever is a *very* long time to be unhappy.

Please Note

I have to remain impartial. As such, I use BCE[4] and CE instead of BC and AD when referring to dates.

[1]Not a bad idea for an end. I shall forward that to the afterlife special effects people and have them cost it out as an option. I'll get back to you by the end of the book.
[2]Amazing how hard these smartypants worked just for a sip of water.
[3]I have great interpersonal skills. Trust me – that's why God chose me for this job. I'm the only archangel who gets to meet *everyone*. Albeit just the once...
[4]Before Common Era.

In the Beginning was the End

*The world began without man, and it will end
without him.*

Claude Lévi-Strauss (1908 – 2009)
anthropologist

Every society has its creation myth[1] – the collective
answer to the child's question "Where did I come
from?" After the elders of the tribe had answered
that one over the night-time fire, the next evening's question would be "Since you're so smart, how's it going to
end?"

The end of the world is nigh! At least that's been the cry
since... since... well, as far back as records go. The first
writing was done on clay tablets in Mesopotamia. Here's
the inscription on one:

*The Earth is degenerating today. Bribery and corruption
abound. Children no longer obey their parents[2]. Everyone
wants to write a book, and it is evident that the end of the
world is fast approaching.*

Assyrian tablet 2800 BCE[3]

That could have been written for this morning's newspa-
pers. Nearly 5,000 years ago, people were reporting almost identical problems to society in the 21st century. Remember – this is amongst the oldest *written* records, so it's
probably the case that people were complaining about

---

[1] Almost all of them also have a Great Flood myth too.
[2] If you're a child reading this book, please understand that's not an order
– it's an observation.
[3] Before Common Era – just a reminder.

corruption and disobedient children right from the moment the development of language made it possible to complain. The only unfamiliar complaint is that *everyone wants to write a book*. Since writing had just been invented, you can imagine it became a craze that swept through society. The old guard would have been complaining about books in the same way that people complained about televisions, computers and the internet – they rot your brain and make your eyes square. The irony is that the author of the tablet was, of course, *writing*. This shows us that unbridled hypocrisy is one of mankind's greatest traits.

But how would book-writing be a danger to society? The answer is that these people wrote on clay tablets. If there were 400 words per clay tablet, then a modern novel would take about 188 tablets, and would weigh more than a large adult man - you'd need a wheelbarrow to carry it. That's a lot of clay. To fire that clay would involve the burning of a huge amount of wood,

so there'd be massive deforestation if everyone wrote a novel. There's no evidence that the Assyrians invented page numbers either, so reading a book could be pretty frustrating. That means you have a lot of angry people with a large number of clay bricks. For all I know there may have been book riots. Could the expression 'To throw the book at someone' really be this old?

Some sources date that quote to 1800BCE, a full millennium later. If this is the case, then books will have become much easier to write, because papyrus had found its way from Egypt to Assyria around that time. However, papyrus would have been hideously expensive and might have caused economic problems for the country if everyone wanted to write. If, indeed, this date of 1800BCE is correct, then it's interesting that the author is writing on a clay tablet. He's not so much a hypocrite as a Luddite who hates the new technology. Of course, he has had the last laugh because all those papyrus books disintegrated a long time ago, and his clay tablet survives. Or he *would* have had the last laugh, but he's been dead for several thousand years and his prediction of the end of the world has proved to be wrong. So now *we're* laughing at *him*. However, if anyone's going to have the last laugh, then you can bet it's going to be God – he'll make sure of that.

This early writing says it all: humans have always been obsessed with the end of the world. Or at least the ones who write books are. If you're reading this, then you're a reader who's at least interested.

But this also tells us something else. It tells us that each generation is convinced that the end of the world is going to happen in their own lifetime. There almost seems to be a collective death wish. Didn't you ever wonder why?

Why do religious leaders insist that the end of the world is nigh?

Social control. For whatever reason, religious leaders want you to believe them, and for you to do what they want – to have children within the religion (to increase market share), and to exert power and influence.

It's also a great problem-solver. If your congregation is having a really bad time of it – persecution, war, famine, economic depression – the end of the world offers an instant fix to any problem:

- Your God smites down your enemies
- Bad/corrupt people are punished
- Your own people get an instant reward, beyond all imagining

So what your religious leader is saying is: "Trust me. Now, give me your money and loyalty and I'll see you're alright. Promise!"

And God's not happy about that, either. In fact, He's somewhat tired of charlatans telling other people what He thinks. He knows very well what He thinks, thank you very much. And if He wants your opinion, He'll give it to you. So that's the other reason He asked me to do this work for Him: He wants you, the consumer, to get the best End Times deal.

> *It is not disbelief that is dangerous to our society; it is belief.*
>
> George Bernard Shaw
> (1856 – 1950)
> playwright

A Note on Nostradamus

No book about the end of the world would be complete without reference to Nostradamus.

Proper name Michel de Nostradame, he was one of the most famous[1] seers who ever lived. Interpreters of his quatrains credit him with having predicted, amongst other things, the Great Fire of London, the rise of Hitler and Napoleon and even – in the text below – the destruction of the twin towers of the World Trade Center on September 11th 2001:

> *In the City of God there will be a great thunder,*
> *Two brothers torn apart by Chaos.*
> *While the fortress endures,*
> *The great leader will succumb.*
> *The third big war will begin when the big city is burning.*
>
> Nostradamus, 1654

In the days after 9/11 that prediction was all over the media. In reality, that fictional quatrain was actually from an essay by a Canadian student called Neil Marshall from Brock University. In 1997 he published that fake quatrain as an example of something which could be interpreted in any way the reader liked. Apparently the line about the third big war was an embellishment by a journalist[2]. What's disturbing is that Nostradamus died in 1566, 88 years *prior* to the date attributed in that prediction – and the press failed to notice. With fact-checking this

---

[1] I said 'famous', and not 'accurate'.

[2] The clue being that Nostradamus wrote in quatrains – i.e. four-line stanzas, and this is a fifth line. Are contemporary journalists really this ignorant?

sloppy amongst professional journalists, is it any wonder the media is ripe for End Times exploitation?

Just for the record, here's another of Nostradamus's quatrains.

> *In the year 1999 and seven months*
> *The Great King of Terror will come from the sky.*
> *He will bring back to life the great king of the Mongols.*
> *Before and after war reigns happily unrestrained.*

July 1999 passed without incident. The only events that might have confused Nostradamus as he looked into the future were:

- Falun Gong, spiritual discipline, banned in China
- India recaptured Kargil from Pakistan
- *Liberty Bell* capsule from the Mercury program raised from the Atlantic Ocean
- NASA crashed the *Lunar Prospector* probe into the moon in the final stage of its search for water
- Megadeth's original drummer, Gar Samuelson died
- *Harry Potter and the Prisoner of Azkaban* released[1]
- *SpongeBob SquarePants* debuted on TV[2]

[1]The book, not Harry and the prisoner. Obviously.
[2]Don't underestimate the significance of this event.

PART ONE

Failed religions

Today is a good day to die.
Crazy Horse (1840? – 1877)
war leader of the Oglala Lakota

I would never die for my beliefs because I might be wrong.
Bertrand Russell (1872 – 1970)
philosopher

I n this section we look at some religions which didn't stay the course, and for whose followers the End Times have come and gone.

The Mayans

Theology: Multitheistic
Followers: Scattered remnants
Geography: Central America
Founded: 2600 to 1600BCE

The Mayans are represented by an angry bloke. He's not smoking a cigar, he's sticking his tongue out at you.

Mayan civilisation may go back as far as 2600BCE, but properly began around 1600BCE with a gradual decline after 900CE. Their civilisation ended completely with subjugation by the Spanish in 1697, after nearly two centuries of warfare.

The Mayans had a so-called Long Calendar. Much has been made of it predicting an end to the world in 2012.

The Mayans were very good astronomers, which is to say that they were able to monitor the slowly-changing patterns in the sky by careful observation. After hundreds of years of observations they noticed what's called the precession of the Earth's axis – the wobbling over a period of 26,000 years like a spinning top. They put the figure at around 30,000 years. They calculated that once every 5,125 years the plane of the sun would appear to intersect with the dark band of the Milky Way (the galactic equator). All of this is, of course, an optical illusion caused by relative movement. They used the dates to calculate the beginning of the last great cycle as having been August 12, 3114BCE.

They assumed that had been the day of the universe's creation. Calculate forward and you arrive at 21st December 2012. They did not suppose this would be a day of destruction – it was American author John Major Jenkins who cre-

The Mayan calendar

ated this myth, because sensationalism sells books. John Major Jenkins now states:

> *In the interest of clarity, I will mention that it would be more accurate to say that the alignment occurs in the ERA of A.D. 2012; because precession is such a slow phenomenon, fifty years on either side of 2012 might be appropriate.[1]*

That's all very well for him to say, now that he's made a fortune from his scare-mongering books.

In 2012 excavations in the Mayan city of Xultún discovered what appeared to be the house of a royal scribe. On his walls he had drawn a calendar extending 7,000 years into the future. Like most ancient civilisations, the Mayans only wanted a degree of certainty about tomorrow.

A final thought on the Mayans. Ask yourself this: why should anyone believe that an ancient society was better than anyone else at predicting the end of the world? After all, they failed to predict their own End Times.

[1]Predicting to one day in +/- 50 years was claiming a 99.997% accuracy.

The Aztecs

Theology: Multitheistic
Followers: None
Geography: North America
(modern-day
Mexico)
Founded: 1325CE

Like their fellow South Americans, the Ma-yans, the Aztecs were pyramid-loving astronomers. Although their civilisation has now passed into history, they deserve an honourable mention due to their End Times accuracy. Few religions can offer such verifiable precision.

Who's a pretty boy then?
The Aztecs had a bit of a thing for dressing up. This guy's dressed as an eagle.

Until the Europeans arrived, there were no horses in the Americas. In South America there were llamas, but they're not as suitable for riding – even a fit llama can only take someone one third of their weight. A large llama will weigh up to 200kg, so they could handle a human up to 70kg (154lbs or 11st) at most – and not for long.

The Aztec priests predicted that the end of their world would be brought by large four-legged demi-gods with the upper half of a man's body on top – what the Ancient Greeks would have described as centaurs. This upper half

21

of a human would be polished silver. These demi-gods would have the power to point at someone and – with a flash and a roll of thunder – kill them from hundreds of feet away. They would also bring plagues which would ravage the population.

In the early 1500s, the priests began to predict that the end of the world was coming in a matter of a few years. As the time drew nearer, their descriptions of the demi-gods became more vivid, and the timing more precise. Indeed, they predicted it almost exactly to the day.

...and then the End of the World was Nigh

The centaurs with the silver bodies appeared from giant sea-faring craft the like of which the Aztecs had never seen. Full of dread and wonder, the priests and nobles went to greet these powerful heavenly creatures, offering gold, silver, luxurious food, and slaves to appease them. The demi-gods took the offerings. Then they pointed at some of the most powerful warriors and – with a flash of lightning and a roll of thunder – those men fell, dead. The demi-gods continued to kill, pillage and rape. Those who were not murdered were struck down by terrible plagues. Within a few years, their civilisation had passed into history; gone forever.

The year was 1512, and the centaurs were – of course – the Spanish Conquistadors. Their silver upper bodies were the armour plate they wore. Wherever the Europeans went they brought diseases to which other human populations had little or no natural resistance.

So how did the Aztec priests predict their own End Times so accurately? Nothing's for certain, but the Spanish were already decimating the islands of the Caribbean after Columbus discovered the Americas in 1492[1]. They almost certainly would have heard descriptions from people they traded with, if not directly, then indirectly.

The Curse of the Aztec Gold

The gold stolen by the Spanish from cultures like the Aztecs and Incas made the Spanish incredibly wealthy. That flood of money led to massive inflation and high population growth, and was invested in non -productive assets – to build magnificent cathedrals and cities, for example. This, combined with high taxes on merchants and manufacturers, meant that the Spanish failed to develop an industrial base and had to import goods. Then the loot ran out. Spain first went bankrupt in 1557, and the once-mighty Spanish empire went into a long, slow decline, from which it has never fully recovered. At the time of writing in 2012, the country is undergoing terrible economic austerity. 500 years on from their invasion and the Spanish are still suffering from the curse of the gold from their South American conquests.

If you want a religion that's 100% accurate about its End Times, then the Aztecs are for you. However, you might want to know a bit about their religious ceremonies before you convert.

Feast days

How about this for a good time? On a feast day you might be selected to be the human incarnation of a god. You will literally be treated like a god, along with a few other lucky fellow-gods. You'll be wined,

[1]Apparently the original inhabitants of the Americas hadn't really discovered them at all. They didn't call them 'the Americas', they called them 'our place'.

dined and worshipped. The downside? At the end of the day you are sacrificed to the real god – you are pinned down on an altar stone, your chest is cut open, your beating heart is ripped out and your body thrown down the temple steps. Your heart is then incinerated. Calling it truly horrific is an understatement.

Pros
- Clear End Times
- Verifiable – they happened

Cons
- Horrific human sacrifices
- Grisly End Times
- No longer on offer, but may be back after the fall of the current civilisation[1]

Summary

One of the most nightmarishly brutal religions in recorded history – you'd be lucky to escape being butchered. Grim end for everyone. On the plus side, you have a 500-year revenge on the people who did it to you. Not that you're there to enjoy it, sadly.

---

[1]Which could be sooner than you think.

Heaven's Gate

Theology: Monotheistic, loosely based on Christianity

Followers: 3?

Geography: California (where else?)

Founded: 1993

The Heaven's Gate logo. At least they put the apostrophe in the right place.

Q: What do you get when a nurse falls in love with a patient with a Messianic complex?

A: Mass suicide

Whatever Marshall Herff Applewhite (the patient) and Bonnie Nettles (the nurse) said about their meeting, at least one reliable witness[1] said they met at a theatre school.

Applewhite, who claimed to have had a near-death experience after a heart-attack, came to believe he was a direct descendant of Jesus[2]. A fortune-teller had told Nettles that she'd meet someone matching Applewhite's description. In turn, she read his stars, and he told her his beliefs.

His first attempt at forming a religion was Human Individual Metamorphosis (HIM). In 1975 he took his follow-

---

[1] One of Applewhite's sons.

[2] Apparently a much easier thing to believe than that you suffered brain damage.

ers out to the Colorado desert to wait for a UFO, which never came.

Nettles died of cancer in 1985. This was quite a big blow to Applewhite, because his creed had been founded on the book of Revelations, from which he had understood that he and Nettles were the two witnesses to the end of the world; that they would die and then be reborn after 3½ days.

In 1993, Applewhite formed a new group Total Overcomers Anonymous (TOA), placing an advert in *USA Today* announcing that that world was about to be 'recycled'. The group was renamed Heaven's Gate after moving to San Diego.

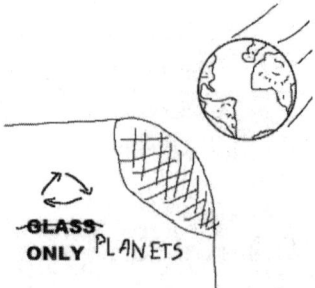

Applewhite and his followers believed that the body was just a container for the soul.[1] He believed that an expedition of higher beings had visited Earth some 2,000 years ago. He believed that he was part of another expedition sent by that alien civilisation, sent in the 1920s. He was the captain of the expedition, and Nettles had been an admiral. He was delighted that people who joined his cult thought themselves to be long-lost crew-members from that same party of higher beings.

---

[1]As do most religions apart from Atheism.

Applewhite had been struggling with his sexuality for a couple of decades, and reportedly spent time in a psychiatric hospital trying to be 'cured' of it. Unhappy at finding himself to be gay or bisexual, but deeply religious, he was celibate – though there are reports that he had had sexual relations with at least one of his male followers. He made celibacy mandatory for all Heaven's Gate members. However, Applewhite went one step further and had himself castrated, as did at least seven others. Bizarrely, in 1996 he spent $10,000 on alien abduction insurance for up to 50 members – this from a cult which believed in their own extraterrestrial origin and destiny. This masks the paranoia that Applewhite had about the earthly authorities persecuting his community.

Comets have long been a magnet for End Times believers, like moths to a naked flame. Having missed the UFO in Colorado in 1975, Applewhite was convinced that he and his crew could hitch a ride on a spacecraft hiding in the tail of the Hale-Bopp comet[1], which was due to come close to Earth in March 1997.

The group numbered 39 at the time of the mass suicides. The first 15 committed suicide on March 24th 1997, with the rest of the group cleaning up after them. On March 25th, 15 more killed themselves. The last nine died on March 26th, with Applewhite third-last to die. The last two to die were women. The means of suicide was apple[2] sauce tainted with phenobarbital, cyanide and arsenic, with a plastic bag tied over the head to ensure asphyxia-

[1]Conveniently, the Hale-Bopp comet has a very long orbital period – thousands of years. Halley's comet is just so passé, with an orbital period of just 75 years. Applewhite was probably the world's first comet snob.
[2]See what he did there? Applewhite, apple sauce. Very egotistical.

tion. The last two women didn't bother with the plastic bags.

All members were wearing the Heaven's Gate armband, with the legend *Heaven's Gate Away Team* embroidered on it. They had changed out of their unisex uniforms into black shirts and sweat pants, with black and white Nike shoes. All lay peacefully on their beds.

If some of this sounds a bit *Star Trek* in its inspiration, then you might be right. Thomas Nichols, brother of Nichelle[1] Nichols – the actress who played Lt Uhura in the original 1960s TV series – was amongst the dead.

One member, Rio DiAngelo, left the group some weeks before with Applewhite's blessing so that he could spread the word. The videotapes he took were made available to the police five years after the event. You can find them on YouTube.

Two former members entered a suicide pact in May 1997, but one survived. He succeeded in killing himself in February 1998. Surviving or new members do keep the Heaven's Gate website up-to-date.

Pros

- Nice uniform, if you like that sort of thing
- Um. That's it.

Cons

- Possible castration (men only)
- Premature death
- Cold and boring afterlife (see overleaf)

---

[1]Yes, that's Nichelle, not Michelle. Don't ask.

Summary

Not a comforting belief-system for the long-term. Great religion for suicidal sci-fi aficionados.

There's a reason I, Nice Mr Death, told you this story. I wasn't best-pleased with Applewhite. He was somewhat surprised – and not to say more than a little disappointed – when I took him to the tail-end of the Hale-Bopp comet and showed him that there was no alien mother-ship. He was even more surprised when I decided to leave him there in the freezing cold and dark for a couple of orbits of the sun whilst he thinks about what he's done. He's lucky that the orbit was reduced from 4,200 years to 2,533 years by a close shave with Jupiter in 1996. Frankly, I'd be within my rights to leave him there forever – after all, that's where he wanted to go in the afterlife. However, when the end of the world comes, I'll shove him in with the rest of you – wherever you are. I like to keep things neat and tidy.

Which reminds me: let's get on with your choice of End Times…

PART TWO

Your choice of religions

Human beings are perhaps never more frightening than when they are convinced beyond doubt that they are right.

Laurens van der Post (1906 – 1996)
writer and explorer

I n this part, I present you with a selection of religions. I've searched high and low to give you as wide a variety as possible. Oh, and *what* a variety…

We're going to judge the End Times of each religion in terms of the following:

- Reliability/Credibility
- Quality of End Times (special effects, etc.)
- The Deal – what do you get after you die
- Proximity – how close are they?

Please remember to focus on the *End Times* of these religions only. Assume you can convert at any time.

Zoroastrianism

Theology: Monotheistic
Followers: 600,000
Geography: Primarily India
and Iran, plus
diaspora
worldwide
Founded: 6000 – 1200 BCE

Hey Mr Tambourine Man
Ahura Mazda

Estimates vary for the origin of this religion. Given that it involves the worship of fire and water, then its real origins probably go right back to the beginning of the fire age, which is around 300,000 years ago. It takes its name from the prophet Zoroaster, who is also known as Zarathustra[1]. In India, worshippers are also known as Parsees (or Parsis). Around 5,000 years ago,[2] Zoroaster demoted a load of other gods and promoted Ahura Mazda to top spot. Ahura Mazda is the only god I know who's got both a first name and a family name.

Zoroastrians believe that life is a fight between truth and falsehood, rather than good and evil – an interesting and thought-provoking perspective.

Zoroastrians see the world as being composed of seven elements: earth, fire, water, wind, plant, cattle, human. Presumably birds and flying insects are part-cattle, part-wind, but I can't say for sure. In the ancient cultures of the

[1]Yes, as in *Also Sprach Zarathustra* – by Richard Strauss, the signature tune of *2001: A Space Odyssey*
[2]No one knows Zoroaster's epoch for certain. Estimates vary from 6000BCE to 100BCE.

West there were four elements: earth, wind, fire, water. Compare that to the Chinese, who believed there were five: earth, fire, water, metal, wood. The Chinese did not have wind – despite all that spicy food.

Mazda cars were named after the god – Ahura Mazda is the god of wisdom, intelligence and harmony. He really is the god of small cars.[1]

There are only about 600,000 practitioners left in the world. In part, this is because the Parsees don't believe in trying to convert anyone from outside the religion.

End Times

Being an early religion, created during a period of progressive civilisation, Zoroastrianism has good, simple End Times.

A comet hits the Earth and there are earthquakes[2]. The mountains get really hot – so hot that all the metal in them melts. The molten metal forms a huge river[3], which everyone has to wade through. Wicked people go through an unspeakably painful purification process in the white-hot metal. However, for good people it feels just like a warm, rejuvenating milk bath. This is a luxury spa day for most of humanity. Zoroaster doesn't mention carrot-juice or massages – but waxing is probably something that happens to wicked people after their painful bath in the liquid metal.

---

[1]His brother Gary runs a Mazda dealership. Mention my name for a discount.

[2]There are always earthquakes in End Times.

[3]Since it's a long river, there's no jostling because there's plenty of room.

The Deal

Cosmic renewal. It's like Heaven on Earth, but not quite. It's as if Ahura Mazda is doing a reality TV makeover show on your life. Your cattle will produce more milk, the roof of your mud hut won't leak and your joints won't ache when it rains. This is a good, solid achievable deal. Sure, it's unimaginative – but the budget is manageable, even in straitened times.

If we were to update this for the modern world, your mobile phone would always have a signal, you'd have perfect Hollywood teeth and no crow's feet, you'd have a shiny new sports car (a Mazda, of course), it would only rain at night, you'd own your own home and there'd actually be something decent on TV.

Famous Zoroastrians

- Persis Khambatta, former Miss World and actress (the bald Deltan woman in *Star Trek: The Motion Picture*)

- Freddie Mercury[1] was born a Parsee

- Homi Jehangir Bhabha – physicist; founder of India's nuclear program (you can see how fire-worship must have influenced his career choice)

- Britain's first three Asian MPs : Dadabhai Naoroji (Liberal), Mancherjee Bhownagree (Tory), Shapurji Saklatvala (Socialist)[2]

- The super-rich Tata family, who made their money in the steel industry – again, fire and molten metal must have been an influence

[1]Liquid metal. See that now?

[2]Notice that these Zoroastrian MPs covered the whole political spectrum easily.

How Close?

Zoroaster was told that there were 3,000 years before the end of the world. Estimates of Zoroaster's date of birth vary from 6,000 to 100BCE. Most scholars now accept a date of 1,000 to 1,200BCE, which means that the end of the world for Zoroastrianism is probably overdue. Given the decline in numbers, that looks about right.

Pros

- Freddie Mercury resurrected
- End Times simple, clear, fair and easy to understand. Only unpleasant if you're wicked
- Cosmic renewal – life gets better

Cons

- Same old life that you had before, albeit much improved

Reliability/Credibility	8
Quality	7
The Deal	8
Proximity	Overdue

Summary

If you're looking for a low-risk, non-scary end-of-world deal, then this could be the religion for you. If you're a fan of legendary rock group Queen, then I assume you've already converted so that you can see Freddie play Wembley Stadium again. In addition to this, you get a life makeover.

Scientology

Theology: Unknown
Followers: Disputed. United States 25,000 to 55,000 in 2001.
Geography: Mainly US[1], UK, other Western Europe
Founded: 1952 (1953 for tax purposes)

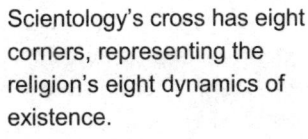

Scientology's cross has eight corners, representing the religion's eight dynamics of existence.

Religious tolerance is at the heart of Scientology – by which I mean they don't seem to tolerate anyone criticising their religion. The world's major religions have mostly moved on from intimidating those who oppose them, but the Church of Scientology has a reputation for employing expensive teams of lawyers to silence their critics.

The founder of Scientology was science-fiction writer L. Ron Hubbard. It has been widely reported that he said words to the effect of "You don't get rich writing science fiction. If you want to get rich, you start a religion."

[1]Particularly Hollywood

"He is a fraud and has always been a fraud. ... My father has always used the confidential information extracted from people during [auditing] to intimidate, threaten and coerce them to do what he wanted, which often meant getting them to give him money. My father routinely used false threats and [information from confessionals] particularly about crimes people had committed to extort money from them. ... My father has always held out Scientology and auditing to be based purely on science and not on religious 'belief' or faith. We regularly promised and distributed publications with "scientific guarantees". This was and has always been common practice. My father and I created a "religious front" only for tax purposes and legal protection 'from fraud Claims'. We almost always told nearly everyone that Scientology was really science, not a religion, but that the religious front was created to deal with the government."

Ron DeWolfe eldest son of Hubbard (born L. Ron Hubbard, Jr.), in an affidavit in Schaick v. Church of Scientology, US District Court Mass., No. 79-2491

Founding myth

75,000,000 years ago Xenu (evil leader of the Galactic Confederacy, in case you didn't know) brought billions of people to Earth in spacecraft resembling Douglas DC-8 airliners, stacked them around volcanoes and detonated hydrogen bombs inside the volcanoes. The Thetans then clustered together, stuck to the bodies of the living, and continue to do so today. Scientologists at advanced levels place considerable emphasis on isolating body Thetans and neutralizing their ill effects.

Although Scientology claims roots going back some 75,000,000 years, it was actually incorporated as a religion in 1953 in the rather unglamorous town of Camden, in the equally unglamorous state of New Jersey. Being a religion allows it certain tax and legal privileges. It has not been granted the same status in European countries, despite lobbying. Followers are alleged to have to pledge a certain percentage of their income to the church, as well as to pay for tuition to reach more senior positions in the organisation.

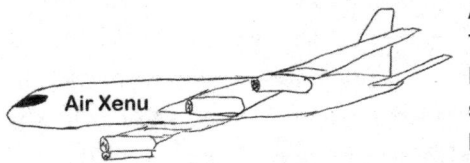

Apparently the Thetans came to Earth in a spaceship resembling a badly-drawn DC-8

Scientology has chosen to pick fights with the psychiatric profession. Tom Cruise famously railed against psychiatry, saying that it should be outlawed. Why would the Church of Scientology want to ban people from getting psychiatric help? Just asking…

Famous practitioners

- Tom Cruise
- John Travolta
- Nancy Cartwright, voice of Bart Simpson
- Kirstie Alley, actress from *Cheers*

The Deal

If you want to do deals in Hollywood, then this is the religion for you. The deal seems to be some kind of reincarnation. Hubbard was known to have had an interest in Hindu mythology. Apparently there are gigantic Scientology symbols etched into the ground at the organisation's base in Trementina, New Mexico. They are to help guide Scientologists from around the universe.

End Times

U nknown. However, if Tom Cruise has anything to do with it, it will involve aliens. He probably viewed his 2005 remake of H.G. Wells' *War of the Worlds* as a bit of a practice run. In fact, fellow Scientologist John Travolta released a film called *Battlefield Earth* in 2000, based on L Ron Hubbard's book of the same name. Set in the year 3000, the human race has been enslaved to the Psychlos (giant aliens) for 1,000 years. The movie was a flop, and the production company went bankrupt.

Pros

- Meet celebrities[1]

Cons

- Quite a few, allegedly
- Expensive. One source put the cost of becoming a Level One Operating Thetan[2] at $300,000
- Credibility

Reliability/Credibility	0
Quality	2
The Deal	0
Proximity	?

Summary

I f you have spare cash and you want to get ahead in Hollywood, this might be the religion for you.

---

[1]In fact, some say that the reason it's flourished as a religion is that it's a good networking group in Hollywood.

[2]Don't laugh.

Islam

Theology: Monotheistic
Followers: c.1.6 billion
Geography: Worldwide
Founded: 610CE

I slam is one of the world's great religions, currently marginally behind Christi-anity in terms of numbers of followers. Just as Christianity is split broadly into Catholics and Protestants, so Islam is split into Sunni and Shia. Of course, it's not as simple as that for either of these venerable religions.

Islam is an Abrahamic[1] religion, which recognises Mohammed as the last in a long line of prophets. The Kabala in Mecca – towards which prayer is directed – was said to have been created by Abraham himself.

The split of Shia Islam from the mainstream happened after the battle of Karbala[2], at which the last of Mohammed's line were killed (this was basically a battle between leadership of the religion on an hereditary basis, or by an elected leader). Shias have been somewhat persecuted following this schism, and so they have a greater tendency towards a catastrophic and end-time view of the world. For many observers Iran, being mainly Shia, has typified this mentality since becoming an Islamic republic.

---

[1] In other words, like Judaism and Christianity, tracing it roots back to Abraham.
[2] Not to be confused with the *Kabala*. Careful with spelling.

The Deal

Islam probably offers the best afterlife deal of any major religion.

For one thing, it offers tremendous reliability. Islamic scholarship was second to none for many hundreds of years. Whilst Western Europe lived in ignorance during the Dark Ages, they kept alive Greek philosophy, astronomy, mathematics, etc.

Here's a list of benefits:

- *Easy to get to Heaven.* "No one shall enter Hell who has an atom of faith in their heart." This is a fantastic deal! Allah is the Most Merciful, and he really doesn't want to send anyone to Hell. You'd really have to struggle not to have at least one atom of faith in your heart, wouldn't you?

- *Tomb with a view.* You get a view of the afterlife from your coffin. Being confined in a coffin until the Day of Judgement could be pretty boring, couldn't it? According to Islamic scholars, you have one view of where you're not going (Hell), and a view of where you are going (Heaven). In-coffin entertainment – invented before LCD screens in the backs of airline seats. Islam is nothing if not innovative.

- *Age guarantee*: 33. Admit it – you've often wondered what age your grandparents will be in Heaven. The answer's simple: everyone will be 33 years old. The prime of your life. Guaranteed, forever.

- *Short waiting time.* The first Christians have now been waiting 2,000 years for the Resurrection and Day of Judgement. (By the way, they don't have in-coffin entertainment to keep them happy.) Now there's nothing anyone can do to hurry up the End Times[1], but you can make it easier. In Islam, your waiting time will feel only as long as the time between your last two prayers. This is a fantastic incentive to pray more – no wonder Muslims pray five times a day. This beats *any* supermarket loyalty scheme.

- *Bunch of grapes upon entering Heaven.* The 72 virgin thing is probably wrong (sorry guys)[2]. It may even be a mistranslation of 72 white grapes. But this is a lovely welcome nonetheless. I bet you'll even find someone's put a chocolate on your pillow.

- *Wine.* There is free, unlimited wine in Heaven. And it doesn't make you so drunk that you make a fool of yourself. Nor does it give you a hangover.[3]

[1]Unless you're a Republican president of the United States.
[2]The Qur'an doesn't put a number on the number of wives (or virgins). This comes from Hadith (tradition) collected by Al-Tirmidhi (died 892 CE) in the Book of Sunan (volume IV, chapters on The Features of Paradise as described by the Messenger of Allah: 'The smallest reward for the people of paradise is an abode where there are 80,000 servants and 72 wives..' And what on earth are you going to do with 80,000 servants? Many Islamic commentators view these assertions as apocryphal, at best.
[3]Sura 56: 12-39

How Close?

number of conditions need to be met.

- *The Mahdi returns.* His birth will take place when there's a solar and lunar eclipse in Ramadan. This happened in 1981 and 1982. Given that the Mahdi will be 33 years old when his rule begins, this could indicate 2014 or 2015.

- *A star with a luminous tail will arise in the East.* All celestial objects appear to rise in the East due to the rotation of the Earth. Halley's Comet – probably the most famous throughout history – last appeared in 1986. A fifth birthday present for the Mahdi?

- *A Muslim in the East will be able to see a Muslim in the West, and vice versa.* Anyone for a Skype call? Together with social media, it played a massive role in the Arab Spring from 2011 onwards.

- *A slave (lady) will give birth to her master.* This is a bit cryptic. The last great slaving nation was the United States. The slaves were black. Although President Obama has no family history of enslavement, I think we're allowed some leeway on this metaphor.

- *When the shepherds of black camels start boasting and competing with others in the construction of higher buildings.* Again, we're looking at metaphors. The shepherds of black camels could be the OPEC members in their black limousines. The world's tallest building is the Burj Khalifa in Dubai.

Given the above facts, the Islamic End Times are looking pretty close. Look around the Middle East in 2011-12 and you see the populations rising up and the Iranians sabre-rattling at the Americans and Israelis over their nuclear programme. If it's not the end of the world, it's certainly the end of an era.

End Times

Islam has a simple, six-point End Time:

- Jesus returns to help the Mahdi
- Jesus breaks the cross and massacres the army of ad -Dajjal (the anti-Christ)
- Peaceful rule established
- The armies of Ya'juj and Ma'juj break out[1]
- The Beast arises
- The Beast is defeated, and the Day of Judgement is at hand

Then it's paradise for everyone, forever.

What could be simpler than that? It's a nice, straightforward ending. Notice too that there's no personal risk or inconvenience on your part. Jesus and the Mahdi sort the whole thing out whilst you sit on the sidelines eating your grapes and drinking your wine.

[1]In Christian terms these are the armies of Gog and Magog. If you're a right-wing American fundamentalist Christian, this means Russia and China.

Possible inconveniences – myths debunked

Most people reading this will be from a Western[1] background, so I realise I have to stray off the End Times a bit here.

- Contrary to popular belief, women do *not* have to wear a veil. That's a matter of personal choice. Nor do men have to grow beards.

- Circumcision is *not* a requirement. As with the veil, that's a cultural choice based on the community you come from.

- Observance of Ramadan. A lot of readers might balk at the thought of having to fast from dawn to dusk for a month once a year – and that includes not drinking any water. However, you can get out of this inconvenience by paying a small fine, or by arranging to do it at a future date.

- Suicide bombing and/or the killing of others. Neither of these is acceptable in Islam, because only Allah (God) can take life. The Prophet Mohammed never killed unless pushed to the limit. Even when his own survival was threatened he was merciful.

- No drinking before Heaven. True.[2]

- No pork, bacon, etc. True.[3]

- Praying five times per day. It's a pillar of the religion, but one many choose to ignore.

---

[1]By which I don't mean cowboys and Indians.
[2]Great health benefit. And imagine never making a fool of yourself at the office party again.
[3]Another great health benefit.

Pros

- Reliability. Arab (later Islamic) scholars kept alive Greek philosophy and literature. They were superb mathematicians and astronomers in their own right. They were also humble – they did not allow their stunning architecture to be perfect, because only God could be perfect. To that end, they would build tiny flaws into their designs.[1] That takes real craftsmanship.

- Easy to get to Heaven – just one atom of faith required[2]

- You're 33 years old in Heaven – guaranteed

- Wine which doesn't give you a hangover

- End Times are straightforward, and not personally dangerous.

Cons

- Looks imminent[3] – 2014 or 2015

Reliability/Credibility	10
Quality	9 (safe, fairly spectacular)
The Deal	10
Proximity	2014-15

[1]Unlike Western architecture from the 1960s, which was flawed in its entirety.

[2]Saddam Hussein was rather counting on that. He ordered an entire copy of the Qur'an written in his own blood during his life, and was reciting passages from the Qur'an when he was hanged. However, some hearts are so black that the atoms of faith just don't stick.

[3]Of course, there are some people who would view the imminence as a pro, rather than a con.

Summary

Going to Hell in Islam is really hard to do – you just have to have one atom of faith in your heart to get to Heaven. Islam gives you an End Time that is straightforward, entertaining, and not personally inconvenient or dangerous. Even if you die before the Day of Judgement, you're guaranteed a short wait and a tomb with a view. Paradise itself is amazing, and it's one of the few religions to specify an age for you and your family, and to guarantee great hangover-free wine.

No wonder Islam is such a popular religion, and continues to grow – this is a fantastic deal, and you'd probably be crazy to turn it down. However, wait beyond 2014-15 and you might not get a chance because your world might have ended.

Judaism

Theology: Monotheistic[1]
Followers: 13.4 million
Geography: Israel 5.9 million, rest worldwide diaspora
Founded: 3760 BCE (earliest possible date), c.1000BCE. Jews put the Creation at 3760BCE[2], making Judaism a bit older than Zoroastrianism

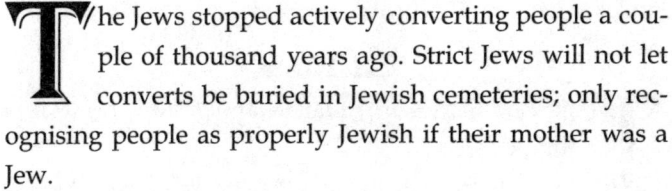

The Jews stopped actively converting people a couple of thousand years ago. Strict Jews will not let converts be buried in Jewish cemeteries; only recognising people as properly Jewish if their mother was a Jew.

Circumcision is a strict requirement. If they discover after your death that you have not been circumcised, they will carry out the ceremony posthumously.

If you're going to be a strict observer of the religion, then there are some bizarre commandments you will have to observe.

---

[1]That's a really, really long time to be faithful to one God. The truth is that they did stray a bit, and God's punished them severely for that.
[2]Christians have spent hundreds of years arguing about the date of Creation. Here's a simple fact: the Jews took dictation from God – they wrote the Bible. Why even bother arguing? Accept the Jewish date and move on. Please.

For example:

- No garments made of mixed fibres. Polyester-cotton mix shirts are out, as are socks with Lycra woven into them, as well as Goretex coats. Not a great religion for wardrobe choice. Presumably Jews cannot go into space, given the mix of materials used in spacesuits
- No drawing, painting or photography permitted
- Shellfish are off the menu
- No trimming of the hair around the temples[1] for men

There are actually several hundred commandments that must be observed – not just the ten that the Christians adopted from the Old Testament. For more, read the Books of Leviticus and Deuteronomy.

End Times

The End Times in Judaism are pretty boring, but totally safe.

First, there has to be 1,000 years of rule by the Messiah. The Messiah is due 6,000 years from the date of creation. That puts the start of the Messianic Era at 2240CE. If you're reading this in 2012, you have 228 years from the date of publication of this book to get ready. Ample warning.

After the 1,000 years of Messianic rule, the world changes to the Garden of Eden or Olam HaEmet – the World of Truth[2]. This change happens overnight. You go to sleep on

---

[1]The temples of your head – not the places of worship.

[2]The World of Truth sounds terrible. Can you imagine a world where everyone told the truth, and there were no little white lies? "Yes, your bum *does* look big in that."

a Friday evening and *This is the way the world ends.*
wake up on the Sab- *Not with a bang but a whimper.*
bath (which is Saturday T.S. Eliot (1888 – 1965)
in Judaism). And then poet
it's the Sabbath forever.

And ever. Which could be really boring. And also rather inconvenient. If you're an observant Jew, you're not even allowed to carry keys or push a pram on the Sabbath. Nor can you do any DIY or drive a car. Okay, you probably don't *need* to do any of those things in Heaven, but what if *your* idea of heaven is DIY and driving?

Except that the Jews are clever. Really clever. You can make something called an Eruv. An Eruv is a set of poles around a community, with a really thin wire – often a fishing line – connecting them. So long as certain rituals are observed, you can do anything you like within the Eruv on the Sabbath. It truly is amazing that the all-seeing, all-knowing, all-present God of Heaven and Earth[1] cannot see past a really thin fishing line. We know for a fact that wearing a hoodie doesn't make you invisible to CCTV cameras, so don't try the fishing line thing if you want to escape justice in the real world. However, if you wear nothing but fishnet stockings whilst committing a bank robbery you might escape mainstream prison after a psychiatric report.

When you get to Heaven you're shown two videos: one of how your life could have been if you'd been good, and another of how it really was. Making you watch that second one is really unnecessary – you know how it was.

[1] The editor thought that using smart words like omniscient and omnipresent would break the flow of words in this sentence. He's wrong: a footnote is much more disruptive.

You didn't just watch the video – you bought the T-shirt and lived the life. If you have to watch it in real time – all 70+ years of it – then you might well rather have been an Atheist and opted out of the afterlife completely. Rabbis have not said whether you can rewind and watch the really good bits of your life time and again, and I doubt you'd be allowed to fast-forward through the bad bits.

The Deal

Given that you enter the World of Truth, there could be a lot of arguments going on around you. However, we'll assume that things settle down after a few hundred years. We'll also assume you've built an Eruv and are free to practice DIY and go rally-car driving.

You get the ultimate pleasure from your proximity to God. The more time you spent studying the Bible during your life on Earth, the closer you get to be to Him.[1]

A considerable percentage of readers will not want to spend their entire lives studying the Bible in the off-chance that they might spend more time sitting around with God feeling fabulous. If that's the case, then your life will continue as before. So, if your life has been about watching football, drinking beer and eating pizza, you will spend all of eternity doing exactly that. Judaic scholars point out that that would be pretty boring. But then they would, wouldn't they?

There is no Hell. However, there is an unpleasant place called Gehenna. It's a bit like a camping trip to North Wales in March. There's also only one pub in the village,

[1]Most Hasidic Jews (the ones who wear black suits and hats) in Israel do spend their entire lives studying the Torah.

and it's not open many hours. The good news is that you will spend no more than 12 months in Gehenna. Indeed, most Jewish people stop praying for the dead after 11 months because they're so sure their loved one has passed on from there. Only five people are going to Gehenna permanently, but I can't publish their names here. Oh, okay – it's Take That. Worse still; they run the pub. Even worse than that; the only track on the jukebox is *Could it be Magic?* If you were to spend the full 12 months in Gehenna you would hear that track 119,454 times – more if it's a leap year. Dire.

Pros

- No Hell – just Gehenna
- Reliability. 100%. Stage one is coming in 2240. These guys have named a date, and you have plenty of time to prepare
- Credibility. 100%. The Jewish people have an excellent reputation for scholarship. Einstein was a Jew
- No nasty End Time. You fall asleep on Friday night and wake up on Saturday morning – couldn't be simpler
- You can continue your life as before – which means drinking and revelry if that was your way
- Terrific comedians. No other religion has contributed such great comedians to the world in proportion to its population: Seinfeld, Jackie Mason, Woody Allen, Sarah Silverman, Peter Sellers, etc.

Cons

- Circumcision (men only)
- Possible over-exposure to Take That if you end up in Gehenna
- Eternal Sabbath (unless you build an Eruv)
- Jewish mother during your life (unless you were a convert)

Reliability/Credibility	10
Quality	4 (no special effects, but safe)
The Deal	5
Proximity	2240

Summary

End Times don't come any safer than this. After-life likely to be stupefyingly boring unless you build an Eruv.

Christianity

Theology: Monotheistic (except that it's not)[1]

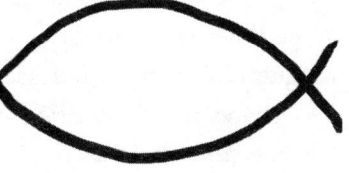

Ichthys – Greek for fish. **ΙΧΘΥΣ** is said in Greek to be an acronym of Jesus Christ, God's Son, Saviour. Or it may refer to the miracle of the loaves and fishes.

Followers: c.2.2 billion, although a significant number are lapsed. Christianity is the world's largest religion by number of followers, though they are split into a variety of sects, or denominations[2]

Geography: Worldwide

Founded: 33CE (assumed)

The world dies over and over again, but the skeleton always gets up and walks.

Henry Miller (1891 – 1980)

writer

*C*hristianity has by far the longest chapter of the book. There are two reasons for this. First, Christians have lot to say about the end of the world.

[1] There's the Father, the Son and the Holy Ghost. Oh, and not to mention the Virgin Mary if you're a Catholic. Then there are the legions of saints you can pray to.

[2] Man goes into a bank and cashes a cheque for £100. "What denomination?" asks the teller. "I don't see what my religion has to do with it!" exclaims the man.

Second, they keep trying to bring it about.[1] In fact, if Christianity wasn't the main religion of the West, it would probably be condemned as a doomsday cult. Imagine if a tabloid newspaper today was to write about a religion that kept preparing its followers for an imminent end of the world, glorified martyrs, and regularly practiced a rite that was ritualised simulated cannibalism. That's what happens in Christianity: during communion[2], the bread and wine are transubstantiated into the body and blood of Christ. For Christians, it is literally true that they are eating the body of Christ and drinking His blood. Even popular hymns contain aggressive lyrics: *Onward Christian soldiers, marching as to war*.

Technically, Christianity is a sect of Judaism. The original Christians were Jews who believed that Jesus was the Jewish Messiah[3]. He was not recognised by the majority of Jews as being the Messiah – just as the latest in a long line of prophets.

Example of the Christians being Jews:

> *How dreadful it will be in those days for pregnant women and nursing mothers! There will be great distress in the land and wrath against this people. They will fall by the sword and will be taken as prisoners to all the nations. Jerusalem will be trampled on by the Gentiles until the times of the Gentiles are fulfilled.*

Luke 21: 23-25

[1] The Europeans tried first, and have now passed the job to the Americans, who have embraced it with enthusiasm.
[2] Many denominations, but not all.
[3] Hence the inscription above his cross saying INRI: *Iesus Nazarenus, Rex Iudaeorum*; Jesus of Nazareth, King of the Jews.

Why are Christians so obsessed with the end of the world?

ood question. The easy answer is that the religion was born during a time of great conflict and hardship. Early worshippers were persecuted by their own kind (Jews), who regarded them as a dangerous cult. The Romans expelled the Christians and Jews from Palestine. They then persecuted the Christians for hundreds of years before Emperor Constantine finally legalised Christianity. (Note that the Empire began its collapse not long after, and that there was a backlash by worshippers of the old Roman gods, who said that this was a punishment by for converting to Christianity.)

Constantine and Christianity

here's a lot more to this than the Christians would care – or dare – to admit. Constantine's Edict of Milan actually allowed the free practice of *all* religions, not just Christianity. He did make contributions to Christianity throughout his life, and was grateful to the Christian God for his success in battle. However, the triumphal arch he built in 315 to celebrate winning the Battle of the Milvian Bridge in 312 was dedicated entirely to the Roman gods.

In the third century CE, the Roman Empire was facing an inflationary crisis: the currency was being debased and the empire was running out of cash. Is it any coincidence, then, that in 331 Constantine ordered the confiscation of all gold, silver and bronze statues from pagan places of worship? These were immediately minted into coins. Even this desperate act failed to halt the currency's decline, and inflation continued. Does this sound at all like the fate of the Spanish Empire following the influx of all that Aztec and Inca gold? Perhaps if the Spanish Conquistadores had read their history they might have been more wary of the curse of the pagan gold. But it's interesting that Christianity's lack of idols (at this stage of its history) made it a favourable choice in inflationary times.

Christianity – what's the attraction?

Christianity adapted itself to local markets. Whereas the Jews gave up trying to convert people to their religion (strict Jews only recognise people as Jewish if their mother was a Jew), the Christians (a sect of Judaism, remember) were willing to compromise. When they moved out of Palestine and into what is now modern-day Turkey, and on into Greece, they dropped the circumcision requirement. They also dropped a great many of the onerous commandments found in the books of Leviticus and Deuteronomy.

The cult of the Virgin Mary was a good counterweight to the female gods found in pagan countries. Christmas was an adaptation of the Roman Saturnalia feast, and of the winter solstice feasts found in other pagan religions. Easter was an adaptation of spring festivals named after the Anglo-Saxon pagan goddess Ēostre. The timing equates to the Jewish festival of Passover (although Constantine stopped the celebration of the Lord's Supper being timed for the day before Passover), and echoes some of the same dietary restrictions. Populations which were used to worshipping myriad minor deities at bridges and springs were given an abundance of saints to take their places – they could continue their superstitious practices as before.

Christianity's biggest selling point is that of instant redemption from sin. All you have to do is repent of your sins from the bottom of your heart, and you're saved.

The Deal

Heaven or Hell – **everlasting**.

This is the first religion we've seen so far where Hell is *everlasting* for the sinner. And it's not just really bad people who go to Hell. The Catholics are great believers in Purgatory, which is place you go to on a temporary basis (but perhaps for thousands of years) to be purified before entering Heaven. St Augustine described the fire in Purgatory as 'more painful than anything a man can suffer in this life'. In short, you don't want to go there either.

The good news about Christianity is the ability to repent, even at the last second. So long as your repentance is heartfelt, your sins will be forgiven and you'll be off to Heaven. This concept is known as 'the stirrup and the ground'. In other words, if you fall from your horse and are able to repent before you hit the ground and die, then you're saved.

Remember that in my official capacity as Death I have met every single human being who has ever died. I can tell you this for a fact: if you lose control of your car at 80mph and hit a brick wall, the last thing that goes through your head is not repentance – it is a brick.

Mark was the first book of the New Testament to be written, which gives it more credibility than the others. It's succinct, and not embellished with as much mythology as the later books. It gives us Christianity's small-print about your prospects of going to Hell.

> *But he that shall blaspheme against the Holy Ghost hath never forgiveness, but is in danger of eternal damnation.*

Mark 3:29

That means anyone who has ever even typed OMG is in danger of going to Hell... forever! That's pretty much everyone.

ABANDON ALL HOPE YE WHO ENTER

OMG! I'm going to hell!! :-((

Come on sunshine, let's be 'aving you!

End Times

In a word: spectacular. Steven Spielberg couldn't do a better job. You name it, it happens. This is gruesome on a truly massive scale and in a variety of ways.

If you want all the gory detail, read the Book of Revelations. Here's a simplified summary:

The Anti-Christ appears and establishes his rule over the Earth. In previous times, people have suggested Genghis Khan, Napoleon Bonaparte, Hitler and Stalin. Today you might think of media-mogul Rupert Murdoch, or perhaps even X-Factor creator Simon Cowell.

The Tribulation. These are the seven years of the Anti-Christ's rule – a really nasty time to be around.

The Battle of Armageddon. This almighty fracas takes place around a place called Megiddo in Palestine. One American preacher, Salem Kirban, suggested that it will be like "...a scene from a Middle Age history book. Bows, arrows, spears, shields everywhere. Crude weaponry but highly sophisticated nuclear explosives for close-up fighting."[1]

The Four Horsemen of the Apocalypse will arrive, each in their turn:

- White (conquest or victory, but often interpreted wrongly as plague)
- Red (war or mass-slaughter)
- Black (famine)
- Green (death[2], bringing Hades [hell] behind him)

The Beast arises (actually there's more than one, but we'll spare you). With ten heads and seven horns, he's pretty scary

The Whore of Babylon rides the Beast

The stars fall from the sky – sounds like a Simply Red record, but it's probably nuclear weapons. At the time of writ-

What's up pussycat? Most people don't know about the 'other' beast – a winged lion. Our big cat looks like he's really spitting feathers!

[1]Salem Kirban founded Second Coming Ministries in 1970. Sadly, he died in April 2010 without seeing the Second Coming he spent 40 years insisting was nigh. Oops.

[2]This isn't me, by the way. This is some fictional Christian death persona. I most certainly don't bring Hades behind me. The Christians are lucky I don't sue.

ing Simply Red thankfully no longer have a record deal, and there is widespread disagreement as to which of these is a worse fate for mankind.

The Heavens are torn off the firmament. Apparently they are rolled up like a scroll of parchment. We're not quite sure what might be behind them. Um, more space and stars, perhaps?

A star called 'poisoned weed' falls from the sky and, well, poisons everything. Poisoned weed in Russian is Chernobyl, interestingly enough. Is it coincidence that the Chernobyl disaster happened in 1986: the same year as the last visit by Halley's Comet? Could this be an indicator that the End Times are already here?

Rivers and seas turned to blood. Some nasty angels come along and pour phials of poison into the rivers and seas to turn them to blood. If you think about this in meta-phorical terms, humans are already doing this. 80% of fresh water in China is now toxic.

Nine-month plague of giant, stinging locusts. These are about five feet high and have three-foot stingers. Tom Cruise clones, perhaps? If you're 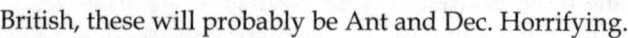 British, these will probably be Ant and Dec. Horrifying.

The armies of Gog and Magog go on the rampage. Who are Gog and Magog? If you're a right-wing American fun-damentalist Christian then that's Russia and China.

Finally, every human being is stuffed into the **Great Wine-Press of God's Wrath**. Then Jesus comes along and tramples everyone like grapes. He tramples them so hard that the blood flows to the height of a horse's bridle for a 200-mile radius.

But it doesn't end with death. No, if your name isn't in the Book of Life, or you don't make the grade because you're one of 'the cowardly, the faithless, the detestable, as for murderers, the sexually immoral, sorcerers, idolaters' then you're cast into the **Lake of Fire**.[1]

After that little lot, you get **1,000 years of rule by the Messiah**, or Christ. If that sounds suspiciously like Judaism that's because it's taken straight from that religion… well, we're back to Christianity being a Jewish sect. This gets around the fact that the coming of the Messiah didn't result in the end of days the last time for the Jews who became Christians.

Revelations Revealed

Pretty grisly stuff, isn't it? The good news is that it's allegorical – no matter what American fundamentalist and TV Evangelists tell you. Indeed, St Augustine (354 – 430CE) in *The City of God* mocks the literal interpretation of Revelations.

The Beast? The ten heads are the ten Caesars of the Roman Empire up to that point in history. The seven horns are the seven hills of Rome. The Whore of Babylon who rides the Beast is a reference to the state of Israel, whose ruling class were – like any other vassal of the Roman Empire – actively collaborating with their rule.

What about the Anti-Christ? That's most likely a reference to a man called Simon bar Giora, who was a revolutionary leader during the First Jewish-Roman War. His popularity made him a figure of fear for the Jewish elders

[1]Revelations 21:8

in Jerusalem, who had rejected him for a position of command after his part in the rout of the Roman army. He struck out on his own, commanding an army of 15,000 with a further 40,000 followers. Effectively, he declared war on the elders, who kidnapped his wife.

Meggido has seen many battles – it is, after all, a fort. If you want to bring it up to date, then the **Battle of Armageddon** happened during WWI. From 19th Sept to 1st Oct 1918 the Allies annihilated a Turkish force.

What about the **Number of the Beast** being 666? Using what is called *gematria* you can (and I simplify here) calculate a number for a person's name. Conceivably it was the Emperor Nero and a reference to a seal that one would need on paperwork in order to pursue trades. You should also note that the Book of Revelations was directed at the people of Lydia, who had just had a heavy tax imposed on them by Domitian (who ruled in Nero's style) when it was written in around 95CE.

Sorry – wrong number?

The oldest surviving manuscript of Revelations actually states the number of the Beast as being 616. Although this is the oldest surviving manuscript, there's no way of proving whether it, or later copies stating 666, are incorrect. But if you had to place a bet, where would you place your money knowing that now?

With regards to the amount of blood produced by the **Great Wine Press of God's Wrath**, if you do the calculations it would require over 28 trillion adult human beings. (See notes after this chapter.) Even if you assumed all of the current seven billion human beings on Earth were adults, you'd need the population of more than 4,000 planet Earths to produce that much blood. And does that really sound like the all-forgiving, loving Jesus you know to be stamping on people until the blood flows out? Well, no – of course not.

We can also do you a **Lake of Fire** if you want. At the time of writing there is one in Ethiopia, caused by the separation into a new continent of that part of Africa. There are currently four other such 'lakes' in the world.

The Rapture

Of course, there has to be a get-out clause from this grisly end for the True Believer. This is what those TV Evangelists sell after scaring you to bits with Revelations. It comes by way of the Rapture, which is part of the doctrine of Dispensationalism. The biblical passage reads:

> *The Lord himself will descend from heaven... and the dead in Christ will rise first....we who are alive and remain will be caught up together with them in the clouds to meet the Lord in the air.*

1 Thessalonians. 4:16-17

This was Paul's first letter to the Thessalonians. He wrote this letter as a morale-booster after visiting them, and you can see he's trying to sustain their hope for better times after the persecution they're undergoing. This is where modern Christians get the idea of Heaven being somewhere in the sky, despite the Bible stating that it will be all around on Earth. Interpretation of this passage led to the development in the 1800s of the doctrine of Dispensationalism. In its basic form, what it means is that any really good Christian has a special dispensation from the Tribulation – i.e. a special note from God that they get free entry to Heaven whilst all hell breaks loose on Earth.

Again, I'm sorry to be a spoil-sport, but the whole doctrine of Dispensationalism is based on a fabrication. Refer to the *Truth about the Rapture* at the end of this section on Christianity.

How Close?

The author of the Book of Revelations was writing contemporaneously, which is a clever way of saying that he was writing as if the events were

In 53CE a rumour spread amongst the Thessalonians that the day of reckoning was at hand. Widespread panic ensued. At this stage, none of the books of the New Testament had even been written.

happening at that time. The same thing goes for St Paul writing to the Thessalonians about the so-called Rapture. In short, it's wishful thinking by men under pressure to deliver results for their believers. They're like impotent politicians promising that things are going to get better, as things get progressively worse. It's quite literally a 'keep the faith' pep-talk. Remember what I explained right at the start about the end of the world being the ultimate victory for you over your enemies?

In order for the End Times to happen, the Jews must spread to the four corners of the world, and the Jewish people must return to Israel. This is why the fundamentalist Christians are so convinced that the End Times are close – the modern Jewish state of Israel was established in 1948. It's why Israel has so many supporters amongst this particular set of people – they see it as their Christian duty to help draw the end of the world as near as possible. Frightening.

In short, the Christians have been heralding the End of Days since the moment the religion was founded, and before the New Testament was even written. They are estimated to have been responsible for over 3,500 end-of-the-world predictions – more than any other religion. So far, they've been wrong every time. Of course, it just needs one of them to be halfway right just once and they can ignore the mistakes of the past.

I will not see the end of the world, nor will you my brethren, for its time is long in the future, 500 years hence.

Pope Leo IX, 1514
Predicted date: 2014

Most recently, the world was treated to Harold Camping, an 89-year-old former civil engineer, and owner of Family Radio – a $100m Christian radio station network. His first prediction was for May 21st 1988. After that failed to happen, he predicted September 6th 1994. In 2011 he made headlines around the world by predicting May 21st for the End Times. Readers may remember news footage of groups of disappointed followers in Times Square, New York as the time came and went. Camping's explanation was that he'd got the maths slightly wrong; that a 'spiritual' judgement had occurred on that day, and that the Rapture was scheduled for October 21st 2011. Many of his believers had sold all their worldly possessions and given the money to Camping to use on a widespread advertising campaign.

October 21st 2011 came and went – the world is still here. Harold Camping had a stroke shortly afterwards, and has not made any further predictions. Given his poor mathematical ability, I would advise the owners of any structures Camping worked on during his career as a civil engineer to have their integrity checked by an expert. I wonder if Camping ever read the parable about the man who built his house on sand?

The truth is that this isn't the first time Fundamentalist Christians have been led up the garden path (or Jacob's Ladder?). In 1840, an American called William Miller predicted the Day of Judgement for October 22nd 1844 (this was after his predictions for March 21st and April 18th of that year had failed to materialise)[1]. His band of followers were called the Millerites (so no problem with ego there, then). As with Camping in 2011, the Millerites sold all their worldly goods and gave the money away, assured of the fact that they'd not need it when they were Raptured up to Heaven. On the night, one Millerite was so certain that the end was nigh that he threw himself off the roof of his barn at midnight, convinced that he'd be caught by angels. He wasn't. I had to pick him up off the ground.[2]

That men do not learn very much from the lessons of history is the most important of all the lessons that history has to teach.

Aldous Huxley (1893 – 1963)
writer

---

[1]You have to wonder if Harold Camping's followers didn't see some kind of pattern here.
[2]Note: Thou shalt not test the Lord thy God. Deuteronomy 6:16, Mathew 4:7, Luke 4:12 How many times do these people have to be told?

How did William Miller calculate an End Time?

He took Daniel 8:14 "Unto two thousand and three hundred days; then shall the sanctuary be cleansed" and took it to mean the cleansing by fire of the Earth by Christ. He used the *day-year-principle*, which assumes that each day of prophecy actually means a calendar year[1]. The starting date was the declaration in 457BCE by Artaxerxes I of Persia to rebuild Jerusalem.

Harold Camping and all the other failed prophets of doom have used similar mathematical work-arounds to try to predict the end of the world. The key thing to note is that they ensure that the date is at hand – you need the immediacy to generate fear to boost your following.

William Miller's failure of 1844 was known as the *Great Disappointment*: if you're going to be a master of exaggeration then you must also master the art of understatement. The movement then split up into several different factions, including the Seventh Day Adventists (who still believe that the Catholic Church is the Beast) and the Jehovah's Witnesses. The Jehovah's Witnesses had a few more Great Disappointments – not including all those millions of doors slammed in their faces each year.

Jehovah's Witnesses End-time prophecies:
1874
1878
1881
1910
1914
1918
1925
1975
1984

Note: it is now forbidden for Jehovah's Witnesses to predict the end of the world.

[1]Mathematical fudges abound. The reason you have to do the day-year -principle is that the original prophecy failed to happen after the specified number of days elapsed. As time goes on, expect the day-decade- principle to emerge.

In 1876 Jehovah's Witnesses Charles Taze Russell and Nelson H Barbour published *Three Worlds*, in which they predicted the end of the world for October 1914: a remarkably accurate prediction of the start of WWI. Close – but no cigar. As the nearby text-box shows, the Jehovah's Witnesses have used a shotgun approach: throw enough predictions out there and maybe – just maybe – one will be right.

In 1704 Sir Isaac Newton made his own statement on the date of the end of the world.

> *This I mention not to assert when the time of the end shall be, but to put a stop to the rash conjectures of fanciful men who are frequently predicting the time of the end, and by doing so bring the sacred prophesies into discredit as often as their predictions fail.*

There's an important distinction to be drawn here: he did *not* predict the end of the world, as so many people mistakenly believe – he stated that it would be *no earlier* than 2060. Few today know that Newton was somewhat of a religious crackpot, and that he spent much of his life dabbling in alchemy. Be that as it may, he was one of the greatest mathematicians who ever lived, and it's interesting that he's trying to use his position to clamp down on doomsayers in his own time.

Christabel Pankhurst would seem the most unlikely of prophets for the Second Coming. Like her sister, Emmeline, she failed to win a seat in parliament after the long struggle for women's suffrage. Instead, she turned to Bible prophecy.[1] She was of the generation which had seen the mass slaughter of WWI. 1925-27 were remarkable years

[1]As you would.

for the forces of Nature so far as Pankhurst and some of the mainstream media were concerned, and they appeared to reach a climax in 1927. There were floods in the Mississippi, New England, continental Europe and China. In Florida, Bermuda and Japan there were hurricanes, tornados and typhoons and even hurricane-force winds in Glasgow and Lancashire. There were earthquakes in: Persia (modern Iran), India, America, Crete, Italy, Portugal, Switzerland, France, southern Germany, California, Australia, Siberia, Alaska, and China – where 100,000 people were reported to have been killed. Britain experienced an earthquake which shook 20 counties plus the Channel Islands.

The end of everything we call life is close at hand and cannot be evaded.

H. G. Wells (1866 – 1946)
writer (quoted from 1945)

To Pankhurst and her ilk, these events seemed like sure signs of the End Times.

As ever, the truth is fascinating, and rather obvious in hindsight. Geology is a relatively new science. Remarkably, the first instrument able to detect earthquakes was invented in China in 132CE by philosopher Chang Hêng. It was a very basic affair, but able to tell from which of eight points on the compass the earthquake was located. The Europeans began developing seismoscopes[1] in the 1700s, but these could only detect local earthquakes.

The big breakthrough came in 1889 when an instrument was finally confirmed as being able to detect an

[1]Yes, seismo*scopes*. A seismoscope will allow you to detect the direction of the source of an earthquake, whereas a modern-day seismo*meter* will also allow you to measure its relative strength.

earthquake on the other side of the world. The technology developed quickly from then, becoming more sensitive and better able to measure the magnitude of the event.

That's one half of the story. The other is the development of the news media. In 1805 it took 11 days for the news about the victory at Trafalgar to reach London. With the advent of telegraph networks, news speeded up somewhat. However, up until 1866, when the first telegraph began operating, transatlantic news was still limited by the speed of a ship (which took weeks to cross).

The BBC began experimental radio broadcasting in late 1922. With this speeding up and increase in efficiency of news delivery, smaller events from around the world would be newsworthy. Up to that point, a devastating earthquake in China having happened weeks or months previously

Good evening. This is the BBC news, bringing you the end of the world. Erm, sorry about that.

would barely have featured as news, since it was an old story by the time it was reported, had no impact on your life, and you knew that the human drama had already played out. However, in 1927 an earthquake killing 100,000 people which you detected on your seismometer and heard about on the radio is front-page news because the plight of the victims is in real-time.

The great floods of the Mississippi in 1927 certainly affected a lot of people – but that's because a lot of people were by then living in areas that were subject to flood; driven there by economic forces. And, of course, this was the first time such floods could be filmed by news companies. They would have sensationalised the footage further to draw crowds into movie theatres. This would have been the first time in human history that moving images of such an event could have been seen by someone who wasn't actually present – a startling fact. For the record, 246 people were killed.

That's swell - the camera loves you!

Compare this to New Orleans in 2005, when over 1,500 people were killed by Hurricane Katrina.

> *And you shall hear of wars and rumours of wars. See that you are not troubled; for all these things must come to pass, but the end is not yet. For nation shall rise against nation, and kingdom against kingdom. And there will be famines, pestilences, and earthquakes in various places.*
>
> Matthew 24:6-7

End Times doom-mongers use the above passage to predict the imminent demise of the world. When have there *not* been wars, or rumours of wars? When in human history have there *not* been earthquakes, famines and disease? This is normality. If the doom-mongers cared to read the text and take the time to understand it, they would realise that Jesus was saying 'all these things must come to pass, but the end is not yet'. In effect, he's telling his disciples not to be panicked by these distractions.

Why do Christians have such a bad track-record?

The first point to note is that Christianity is the largest religion in the world, and that it's split into a very large number of sects; some of them quite extreme in terms of their distance from other doctrines (or, indeed, Jesus's preaching).

The second point is that Christianity has spread into a very diverse set of societies, and at very different times in the development of those societies. Each society has brought its own beliefs to the religion.

Third, unlike the Qur'an, there was no single author[1], and accounts were written over a long period – none of them probably less than 70 years after the death of Christ.

The Jews were responsible for writing the Old Testament, and spent many hundreds (if not thousands) of years revising stories from an oral tradition. The Jews were just writing for a Jewish audience. The New Testament has dozens of authors, each of whom is writing at a different time, and for a different audience. That means it's prone to a variety of interpretations, and that anyone can come along and make their own theories work.

In order to get to the four books of the Apostles which most Christians accept today, a great many texts were discarded. Various councils would have met to approve these different compilations, and the contents would have been selected to suit the needs of the community and church at that time. It is not this book's remit to discuss them here, but numerous texts survive. At the time of Emperor Constantine's formal acceptance of Christianity, some estimates put the number of books as high as 600. Were it for a different decision from some ancient com-

[1]Although the Hadith do have a number of authors.

days to the End Times. Of course, that didn't stop tens, if not hundreds of thousands being slaughtered in Europe during the Thirty Years War in the 17th century. But that was a straightforward fight between mainstream Catholics and Protestants, rather than doom-mongering sects – which apparently made it perfectly acceptable.

Africa has had its share of tragedies, though they are under-reported. One you probably didn't hear about was the Movement for the Restoration of the Ten Commandments of God, in south-west Uganda. It was founded around 1994 by four excommunicated Catholic priests, two nuns and an alleged former prostitute. The true death -toll will never be known, but it's thought that around 1,000 men, women and children were killed or committed suicide around March 17th 2000 – the day when the cult's leaders said that the Virgin Mary would return. An accurate forensic analysis of the scenes of the deaths will probably never be available, but it appears that many victims may have been lured into a church, its doors nailed shut, and the occupants burnt alive.

When they get it wrong there's always an explanation for the delay. The Christians are worse than buses – probably three ends of the world will come along at the same time. Hitch up with the wrong branch of Christianity and your leader might just make the end of the world happen for you sooner than you want.

Pros

- Instant redemption at point of death – so long as you a) remember, b) have the time, and c) make it heartfelt

Cons

- Really horrible End Times, drawn out over a period of years
- Near certainty of everlasting Hell – Purgatory at the very least
- Sharing Heaven with Christians (if you get there)
- No in-coffin entertainment, unlike Islam
- Real-time death experience: 2,000 years in your coffin will feel like 2,000 years, unlike Islam
- Completely unreliable: long history of botched End Times

Reliability/Credibility	1
Quality	10 Spectacular, but horrific
The Deal	1 Near certain hell
Proximity	?

Summary

G iven the above, Christianity in its purest and most literal form doesn't appear quite so appealing as it's cracked up to be. There are long and hard End Times to endure. There's a near-certainty of either everlasting Hell, or enduring horrific pain for an unspecified amount of time in Purgatory. Furthermore, it's quite clear that Christians simply cannot do basic maths. When it comes to the End Times, they do promise to stage a spectacular show. However, they fall over badly when it comes to putting a time on it.

Christianity – it's not all bad

I t's already happened – a belief or doctrine called Preterism is widely held. Most Christians don't believe that the Book of Revelation is literal. Indeed, many of them recognise it as a work that was contemporaneous to its time, and that the major prophecies have come to pass. As we saw in the *Revelations Revealed* section, we saw that the Beast and the Whore of Babylon are easily explained as allegory.

Mainstream churches – such as the Catholic, Orthodox and Anglican churches – don't talk in Apocalyptic terms; nor do they predict the end of the world. It's the new and the radical who seek to scare-monger believers into a certain course of action and gain followers.[1]

[1]Not to mention cash, political power, etc.

Christianity – Important Notes

The Truth about the Rapture

A Jesuit priest from Chile, Manuel Lacunza, wanted to stop the Roman Catholic Church being slated as the Anti-Christ by Protestants. He published a work under the pseudonym Rabbi Juan Josaphat ben-Ezra, the main thrust of which was that the Anti-Christ's rule would only last 42 months (three-and-a-half years). Given that the Roman Catholic Church by then had been around for over 1,400 years in one form or another, then it couldn't possibly be the Anti-Christ.

Lacunza had come to Spain from Chile. After King Charles III expelled the Jesuits from Spain and its colonies in 1767, he was exiled to Italy. Pope Clement XIV briefly banned the Jesuits from the sacrament, then in 1773 – under pressure from France and Spain – he dissolved the Jesuits completely. Lacunza was now no longer a priest, and at this point he adopted millennialism. He published a 22-page booklet called *The Anonymous Millennium*, which was widely circulated in South America, against his wishes. He was denounced to the Inquisition. In 1790 he completed a three-volume work *The Coming of the Messiah in Glory and Majesty* (*La venida del Mesías en gloria y majestad*). The work was printed around ten years after his death, and in 1819 the Inquisition ordered it removed from circulation. It was put on a list of prohibited books in 1824 by Pope Leo XII.

In 1816, the founder of the Catholic Apostolic Church, Rev Edward Irving, was so impressed by the book he translated it and published it in 1827 as *The Coming of the Messiah*. John Darby picked the idea up from there and developed the idea of the Rapture and Dispensationalism – i.e. that pious Christians will be exempt from the Tribulation. Darby went to the US, where his ideas were largely rejected.

The story turns to Cyrus Scofield. Scofield had been a minor state politician in Kansas, and a heavy drinker who abandoned his family. He resigned from public office after a scandal involving bribery and forgery, and probably spent time in jail. He converted to evangelical Christianity under the influence of a dispensationalist preacher and after a few years of preaching began to style himself as Reverend, although no records exist of his having been awarded a Doctor of Divinity degree.

His *Scofield Reference Bible* contained notes on dispensationalism and premillennialism, and became a huge influence on American Christian fundamentalist thinking. The royalties were substantial, and he used them to found a biblical university in Pennsylvania and the Dallas Theological Seminary. It is this latter institution where most of the TV Evangelist preachers are, for want of a better word, educated – and where they are inculcated with their beliefs about the proximity of the End Times.

This whole doctrine originated from the state persecution of a Jesuit priest in the late Eighteenth Century. It has echoes of early Christian writings, which were also formed during a time of state persecution. It serves TV Evangelists well, keeping their flocks compliant. That it originated with a Jesuit priest from the Catholic Church is not something they readily acknowledge.

Christians Can't do Maths[1]

The Great Wine Press of God's Wrath

For a 200 mile radius, blood poured to the height of the horse's bridle.

Revelation 14:20

To make the calculations easier, I've converted into the metric system. A horse's bridle is about five feet (1.5m) from the ground. An adult human contains c.5.5l of blood.

$1m^3$ = 1,000 litres (l)

h = 1.5m

r = 1,609.344 x 200 = 321,868.8m

Area (a) = πr^2 = (22 ÷ 7) x 321,868.8 = 103,599,524,413.44m²

Volume = a x h = 103,599,524,413.44 x 1.5 = 155,399,286,620.16m³

= 155,399,286,620,160 litres of blood

155,399,286,620,160 ÷ 5.5 = 28,254,415,749,120 humans

The population of the Earth is thought to have reached 7,000,000,000 in October 2011, so the amount of blood needed would require 4,036.35 populated Earths.

I've been generous in my calculations by assuming that the human population is entirely adult. However, around 30% of the population is under the age of 16 and will not have 5.5l of blood. The number of humans required would be much higher, and the number of Earths greater as a result.

---

[1]American readers please note that it's *maths*, not *math*. The subject is *mathematics*.

More bad Christian maths

In the early church, bishop (later saint) Papias, who was a friend of John the Apostle, stated:

The days will come, in which vines shall grow, each having ten thousand shoots, and on each shoot ten thousand branches, and on each branch again ten thousand twigs, and on each twig ten thousand clusters, and on each cluster ten thousand grapes, and each grape when pressed shall yield five-and-twenty metretes of wine.

Let's do the maths for just one vine:

10,000 branches, 10,000 twigs, 10,000 shoots, 10,000 clusters, 10,000 grapes = 100,000,000,000,000,000,000 grapes.

Each grape bears 25 metretes of wine. One metrete is 37.4 litres.

Total volume of wine = 100,000,000,000,000,000,000 x 25 x 37.4 = 93,500,000,000,000,000,000,000 litres, or 9.35×10^{22}.

Assuming wine to have the same density as water, that's 9.35×10^{19} tonnes.

For comparison, the mass of the Earth is 5.9736×10^{21} tonnes.

So the grapes on one vine are 1.57% of the mass of the Earth.

The total mass of the hydrosphere is 1.4×10^{18} tonnes. Assuming wine and water have the same density[1], the grapes from just one vine will yield a volume of wine about 66.8 times the volume of all the water on Earth (oceans, rivers, lakes, puddles, clouds and even in plants and animals). I can only suggest that there's been a really

[1]The mass of the hydrosphere is calculated as being the mass of the water in the sea minus the salt. You'll have to try much harder than that if you want to catch me out.

terrible mistake and that this was the original intended use of the Great Wine Press of God's Wrath.

Of course, Papias tells us that John the Apostle told him this, and that John says he heard it off Jesus. I think Papias realised he'd got the maths very badly wrong on this, and tried to pass the buck. Very, very poor form to try and pass the buck to Jesus. Possibly even a mortal sin.

He then gets carried away and says this about grain:

> Likewise also a grain of wheat shall produce ten thousand heads, and every head shall have ten thousand grains, and every grain ten pounds of fine flour, bright and clean.

The short answer is about 453,720 tonnes of flour. You can do the maths yourself. Assuming you're not a Christian, of course.

Buddhism and Hinduism

Theology: Multitheistic, but also pantheistic[1]

Followers: Buddhism 500million, Hinduism 1billion[2]

Geography: Originally Indian sub-continent, Indo-China, Far East, then worldwide after 1960s (diaspora and hippy movement)

Founded: 600 – 400BCE (Buddhism), 1700 – 1100BCE (Hinduism)

The *Dharmachakra* (above) represents the Noble Eightfold Path of Buddhism. Probably where Scientology got its eight 'dynamics of existence' from.

Aum or Om, the mystical sound which is common to both Hinduism and Buddhism

[1]God permeates the universe.

[2]Buddhism is often viewed as a triple religion, incorporating Taoism and Confucianism. If these were included in the numbers, it would total 1.9bn. However, these latter two are more humanist in nature and technically do not have a God at their centre.

What the caterpillar calls the end of the world, the master calls a butterfly.

Richard Bach, (1936 –)

writer

Buddhists and Hindus believe in reincarnation, so I've put them together.

They're just not playing the same game as the rest of you. Thankfully, I managed to automate the whole process when it was invented, so I don't have to take bad people from dying to being reincarnated as beetles – nor do I have to take them from rabbits to cattle. It's all done by a clever algorithm – easy when you have guys like Pythagoras, Newton and Alan Turing to work with.

End Times – Hinduism

The contemporary view[1] amongst Hindus is that each Divya Yuga (full cycle) consists of four yugas, and lasts 4.3 billion years (the age of the Earth is approximately 4.5 billion years). The yugas are as follows:

Yuga	Duration	Characterisation
Krutha Yuga	1.632 billion years	Humans are heavenly bodies
Treta Yuga	1.3 billion years	Silver age
Dwarpa Yuga	884 million years	Bronze age
Kali Yuga	448 million years	Iron age

[1]Refreshing that one of the oldest religions keeps up with current cosmological thinking.

The human race is now in the Kali Yuga – the age of hypocrisy and quarrel.

The life-span of humans in each yuga gets reduced. In the Krutha Yuga it is a few thousand years but in the Kali Yuga (the present age) it is about 100 years.

When one Divya Yuga (full cycle) is completed, the universe contracts to the size of a particle of dust[1]. Then there is a big bang and the new cycle begins.

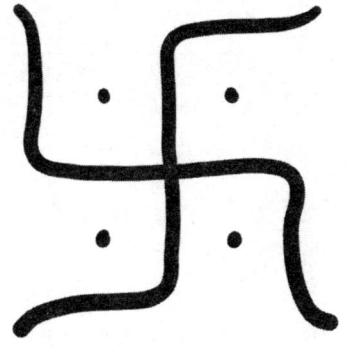

The urban myth is true. The Nazis stole the swastika from Hinduism – though it's found in many ancient religions around the world. In Sanskrit the word 'svastika' means 'to be good'.

Summary

As I said at the start, it's not really playing by the rules because there are no real End Times. However, they do get points for recycling. Hinduism gets bonus points for having written the *Kama Sutra*.

---

[1]Ah, there's the crunch I was talking about in the Introduction. No need to get a costing from the special effects people – if you want one we can just borrow it from the Hindus. Looks like they won't be needing it for a while.

Atheism

Theology: Multitheistic, pantheistic (brands, property, money)

Followers: 300m-500m

Geography: Worldwide. More vocal in Western democracies. Eerily quiet in theocracies such as Iran

See what they did there? Those clever Atheists do subversive humour[1]

Founded: Immediately after first religion, making it the second-oldest religion in the world[2]

It isn't necessary to imagine the world ending in fire or ice there are two other possibilities: one is paperwork, and the other is nostalgia.

Frank Zappa (1940 – 1993)
singer-songwriter

An atheist is a man with no invisible means of support

John Buchan (1875-1940)
novelist

Atheism is a religion that's growing in popularity and becoming more militant by the year. Indeed, it seems to have become a religion in itself. Don't believe me? Harvard University has had an

---

[1] With no afterlife to look forward to, they have to take every chance.
[2] Think about it.

atheist chaplain since the 1980s, and most other American universities also have them. British universities are following suit. There is the First Church of Atheism which – at the time of writing – has over 5,200 ordained ministers.[1] This organisation even wants to buy a church building. To do *what*, exactly? Is this a case of steeple-envy?

There seem to be three main streams, or sects, of atheism. The first is a group of people who simply don't believe in any kind of God or religion and don't belong to a formal group. The second is a kind of atheist who will organise themselves into a group like the Humanists, and will carry out ceremonies of a non-religious nature to mark important events – a remembrance service for a dead person, for example. The third seems to be a kind of militant atheist – the antithesis of the holy warrior or Jihadist. They campaign against religion, seeing it as an aberrant behaviour that needs to be rooted out.

[1]Ordained to do what, we don't know. Nor, it would appear, do they.

End Times

O f all the religions, Atheists have the widest palette to choose from. Furthermore, as mankind's understanding of the universe expands, the possibilities become ever-more incredible by the year – they're not stuck with boring old earthquakes and comets. For example, they could have:

- Solar flares
- Plague – virus or bacterial
- Meteorite/asteroid impact[1]
- Gamma ray burst[2]
- Death of bees causing a food crisis
- Super-volcano
- Massive solar flare
- Ice age
- Nuclear war
- Americans with bad maths[3]

However, the reality is much more mundane. In 2003, Professor Sir Martin Rees, English[4] Astronomer Royal, was asked for his views about the end of the world. He said that there was a 50% chance of it happening within the next 100 years. He gave two likely scenarios:

[1]In 2012 Nasa estimated that there are over 4,700 asteroids over 100m in diameter with orbits taking them within 5 million miles of Earth. Only a quarter have been identified so far.

[2]This is cool. A dying star explodes within a few hundred light years of Earth, emitting gamma-ray radiation so powerful as to kill every living thing, down to a depth of half a mile in the ocean. As the Earth rotates during the day, like a giant gamma-ray rotisserie, those previously protected by the mass of the Earth will become exposed to it. This would put evolution on the Earth back hundreds of millions of years. Larger creatures at the bottom of the sea would do well for a short period, gorg-

1. Technological breakdown

2. Slow environmental change

Pathetic. No, let me rephrase that: *absolutely* pathetic. The man's an eminent astrophysicist – surely he could do better than that? It means that anyone could simulate the Atheist end of the world in the comfort of their own home: simply unplug your internet connection and turn up the central heating. Of all the End Times, Atheism has the most unimaginative and least exciting. There's not even a definite cut-off point.

Doomsday Clock

In 1947 the board of directors of the *Bulletin of the Atomic Scientists* at the University of Chicago made a symbolic clock face to indicate mankind's proximity to the end of the world. The first setting was at seven minutes to midnight.

Why is it constantly set to just before midnight? Why can't it be set to ten in the morning, with 14 hours to go? If it's 23:55, then we're 99.653% of the way through the day. Any decent scientist or mathematician would see that as either rounding or experimental error.[1]

ing on the dead matter. However, the sheer volume of rotting material would rob the sea of oxygen, killing higher species. Something very like this happened when the ocean currents stopped flowing. Nasty.
[3]Seriously. On September 23rd 1999 Nasa's Mars Climate Orbiter crashed because ground-based software fed it instructions in pound-seconds instead of Newton-seconds when it was decelerating. If Nasa don't know Imperial from Metric, God help the rest of America.
[4]English, not British. Scotland has a separate Astronomer Royal.

[1]This is as bad as the Mayan calendar nonsense from John Major Jenkins. Shame on these scientists.

The Deal

Nothing. *Nada*. *Pas de Rien*. A big fat zero. There is no Heaven, no life after death of any sort. Your consciousness ceases and you wink out of existence.

Are you *really* sure you want to choose Atheism?

Pros

- Do anything you like in your life, with little or no guilt
- No dietary or alcohol restrictions

Cons

- Your Atheist friends may treat you badly, since there's no commonly agreed moral code
- Difficult to find meaning in your life
- Poor health: obesity, type II diabetes, alcoholism, drug-addiction
- Unimaginative End Times
- No clear time-line, and no one in charge
- No community spirit
- No eternal life

Reliability/Credibility	1
Quality	0
The Deal	0
Proximity	50:50 by 2103

Summary

Believing in nothing is an easy option. However, believe in nothing and that's exactly what you'll get. You have been warned. If you really do want to choose this option, I suggest you at least consider adopting Confucianism or Taoism – that way you'll at least have some moral guidance. You probably don't want to choose the celibacy practices.

PART THREE

Choosing your End of the World

Don't worry about the world ending today. It's already tomorrow in Australia.

Charles M Schulz (1922 – 2000)
cartoonist of *Peanuts*

The day the world ends, no one will be there, just as no one was there when it began. This is a scandal. Such a scandal for the human race that it is indeed capable collectively, out of spite, of hastening the end of the world by all means just so it can enjoy the show.

Jean Baudrillard (1929 – 2007)
philosopher

Are You Ready?

Count no man happy till he is dead.
> Solon, (638 – 558BCE)
> father of democracy

In the long run we are all dead.
> John Maynard Keynes (1883 – 1946)
> economist

What men want is not knowledge, but certainty.
> Bertrand Russell (1872 – 1970)
> philosopher

What have we learnt? We've learnt that there are always an awful lot of people out there trying to predict the end of the world. This goes as far back as records exist. Each generation throws up its batch of doom-mongers, who will usually exploit the poor and ignorant by promising them Heaven on the basis of the reworking of some nonsensical prophecy written by a bunch of long-dead people who indulged in wishful thinking during some bad times. Ask yourself what's in it for them, and what they want from you. Bertrand Russell (above) is right: people prefer certainty to knowledge. Certainty is the appeal of the End Times, and makes them easier for religious leaders to sell during uncertain times.

In fact, both the Bible and the Qur'an state that "No man knoweth the hour or the day", and it is a sin in Christianity and Islam to predict the end of the world: that is God's business. Believe me: you'll *know* when God's decided.

Einstein said that "God doesn't play dice." He was talking about particle physics here – but if God is hiding somewhere, isn't he in this weird universe[1] that includes the aptly-named God Particle?

Dice have no memory. Just because the Earth is hit by a cataclysmic event on a regular cycle doesn't mean that the cycle is running to a definite timetable.

Why not take *Pascal's Wager*? Blaise Pascal, the French philosopher, had the idea that it might be wise to invest some time in a religion on a casual basis as a hedge. That's a pretty good idea – very clever, for a Frenchman.

So far as your physical body is concerned, remember that any element heavier than carbon can only have come from a supernova – the massive explosion of a star. That means the key elements that make your body are star-dust, and that you are born of the stars. You have already been through the most devastating explosion the universe can deliver, and you have been reborn from it.

Whichever religion's End Time you choose, please don't lose focus on your actual life. If there's one thing I hate it's when I have to take someone to the afterlife who realises that they've not made the most of life on Earth. Get out there and enjoy it while you can!

The fear of death follows from the fear of life. A man who lives fully is prepared to die at any time.

Mark Twain 1935 – 1910)

writer

Finally, I hope it's a very long time before we meet on a professional basis.

Thank you for reading,

Nice Mr. Death

---

[1]Or multiverse. I'm not telling...

PART FOUR

Tales from the Afterlife

*What I've said that turned out to be right will be con-
sidered obvious, and what was wrong will be humorous.*
Bill Gates (1955 –)
entrepreneur and philanthropist

How Hell was created

When they die, a lot of people ask me how and why Hell came into being. Here in print for the first time, I tell you the real inside story.

After God made Heaven and Earth we had a big staff meeting. As you know, Lucifer tried to carry out a board-room putsch. He was a typical MBA-type, actually. You know the sort: always mouthing-off about case-studies, but no actual on-the-job experience. I mean, where was Lucifer when there wasn't even a universe? Talk about ingratitude. Can you believe he actually told God that he just 'hit lucky', and that he'd got the 'core proposition' wrong because he hadn't done the research? None of us would have been in that room if the Boss hadn't decided to set the operation up in the first place.

If there's one thing God's got in abundance, it's a sense of fair play[1]. He told the uppity Lucifer to go and design a third domain for himself, because clearly there wasn't room for two strong managers on the team. God said He'd even build it for him if he wanted – the deal being that he and his mates would have to go and live there.

So Lucifer and his know-it-all buddies went away and drew up all these fancy blueprints. Believe me, they looked absolutely spectacular, and there were those amongst the angels still loyal to God who had second thoughts. The Boss took a look at the plans. You should have seen Lucifer's chest swelling with pride as God turned them this way and that, occasionally grunting or sucking his teeth.

[1]Really, you have no idea what a great boss he is.

"Some very clever stuff going on here with the maths, Lucifer[1]," said the Boss.

"Of course," snorted the arrogant archangel. "Your equations are, frankly, rather simplistic. My boys and I have run my algorithms and they are *so* much more efficient – you get out ten times as much as you put in."

"Ten times as much for no extra work, eh?" God let out a whistle. "And you're sure these…. let's call them *derivatives*, really track the underlying reality efficiently?"

"Absolutely," said Lucifer. "It would take a million-sigma event to throw them off even just a touch. It would take an infinite amount of time for that to happen. Now, keep your part of the bargain and create my third domain for me, *if you'd be so kind*."

"Of course," said the infinitely kind God. He commanded it to be so, and the third domain flashed immediately into being. There wasn't a single one of us who wasn't impressed by this state-of-the-art domain. Being omnipresent, we were all instantly able to look around the whole thing. To use your human parlance, *it rocked*. It had the spiritual domain equivalent of leather bucket seats and a turbocharged engine, if you can imagine that[2].

"Any of you losers want to join the rest of us?" asked Lucifer, withdrawing his omnipresence from Heaven. I'm not going to say who it was[3], but I saw one of the guys twitch. "No takers? Well, enjoy eternity in boring-old Heaven. Goodbye." The door between Heaven and the third domain slammed shut with a noise that reverberated

[1]Yes, we did occasionally call him Lucy. God didn't.
[2]Which of course you can't. Sorry. But be patient – you'll know it after you die.
[3]Uriel knows.

around the universe.

I cleared my throat. "Boss?" I asked.

"Yes, Thanatus[1]?"

"He's not that bright, is he? He said a million-sigma event would take an infinite amount of time to come around. And then the last thing he mocked us with was enjoying eternity in boring-old Heaven."

God smiled and slapped me on the back[2]. The other lads realised what I was on about and within a few seconds we were all falling about with laughter.

Time was young back then, and hadn't settled down into the linear state that you humans experience now[3], so it wasn't long before an infinite amount of time had run through the algorithms[4]. Of course, we'd never have known it had passed because Heaven was running on reliable, old-fashioned maths: the real stuff.

What alerted us to an infinite amount of time having passed was the large explosion from next door as the derivatives blew up as, not one, but an infinite number of million-sigma events happened[5].

It is the echo of that Big Bang that astronomers are able to detect at equal levels no matter where they look in the universe. Just as Heaven is all around you, so is the echo of the creation of Hell.

[1]That's my name.

[2]It's not just my great interpersonal skills that got me the job. God needed someone who could do the maths needed to be everywhere in the space-time continuum at once.

[3]Or, rather, *believe* you experience.

[4]This is mind-bending stuff if you're not used to it. Don't ask a Christian to explain the maths. Or an investment banker.

[5]That's what happens with infinity – you give it something infinitely impossible to do and it'll do it for you an infinite number of times.

The faulty derivatives? They live on too. After Hell blew up they were released into the universe. Lucifer put them to work in the investment banking industry. Do you think it's a coincidence that there are so many people educated in theoretical physics and astrophysics in the banks? The mysteries of God's creation attract some of the finest minds, and the echo of the Big Bang was infested with bad maths, so it infects their minds with delusional ideas. It's probably why some of them think they're 'masters of the universe'.

Once they get the maths right they'll realise they don't need the illusion of Lucifer's Dark Matter to balance the books.

My favourite story about me

Don't fear the Reaper

Blue Öyster Cult
Rock Group (1967-)

A wealthy merchant was in the market square in Damascus one morning when he bumped into me. We both jumped back in surprise. "My apologies," I said, recovering my composure. "I'm actually coming for you tomorrow. Enjoy your day."

The man screamed in terror, ran away and hid in his cellar. He sent his most trusted servant to bring him the wisest man in Damascus.

"I saw Death in the market today," he told the wise man. "I seem to have caught him unprepared and was able to run away to the safety of my cellar. But he said he's coming for me tomorrow. How can I escape him?"

The wise man thought for a while, then gave the merchant his answer. "You must find the fastest horse in the city and ride it overnight to Aleppo. You must reach the market square before dawn."

"But that has never been done during the day, never mind at night!" said the merchant.

"That is the only way you can escape Death," said the wise man, and left.

The merchant immediately went to the greatest stable in Damascus and spent his entire fortune on the fastest horse ever to have been bred in the city.

Without stopping to bid his family goodbye, he rode straight for Aleppo. He rode hard all through the night on the deserted road, whipping the horse on. When he was ambushed by brigands he rode straight at them, scattering them on the road. They gave chase but their horses were no match for his steed. He drove the horse on relentlessly, and by the time he reached the outskirts of Aleppo there was a faint glow in the East. The horse staggered into the market square, collapsed and died. The sun was not yet up – the merchant had done it! He cried out in joy at his victory over me: Death.

I tapped him on the shoulder and asked him to follow me to the afterlife. Just then, the first rays of sun lit up his exhausted face.

He threw down his cap in despair. "I was told that I could escape you by riding overnight from Damascus, and that you would never catch me if I reached the market square at Aleppo before sunrise."

"You learnt the lesson in life very late: wise men are often wrong. Now, let's be going."

"Before you take me, tell me one thing."

"Of course," I said. "What would you like to know?"

"What I don't understand is why you were surprised to see me in Damascus yesterday."

"Simple. I was expecting to see you here today before dawn. I couldn't see how you were going to make it."

Hardworking, firm and fair – but with a *great* sense of humour[1]. I consider *myself* successfully rebranded.

---

[1]And, I admit, a bit of a pedant,.

Resources

The resources for this book are held online at the address below. This book is based on *The End of the World Show*.

For more information, videos, links to weird and wonderful things, and to find what's new in the End Times, please visit:

www.endshow.com

There's plenty more writing and performing on:

www.markspeed.co.uk

Some of which you might find a little rude, and some of it rather stimulating.

Acknowledgements

This book is based on *The End of the World Show*, www.endshow.com, performed in Edinburgh on PBH's Free Fringe in 2011 and 2012. I am grateful to Peter Buckley Hill for giving the show a performance space, and for the legions of volunteers who make the Free Fringe possible. www.freefringe.org.uk.

The show's director, Chris Head, is one of this country's great unsung comedy heroes. His expert guidance made all the difference: www.chris-head.com.

My sincere thanks also to Murray D.E. Henderson for his support and encouragement, and also to Doug Trueman and The Rev[1] for their proof-reading.

Last, but most certainly not least, thanks to my parents Hugh and Joan for their kind hospitality during the Fringe.[2]

[1]The Rev didn't proof the bits on Christianity, though.
[2]And for so many other things.